Christ's Last Order

Christ's Last Order
Copyright © 2017 Derek Prince Ministries – International.
This edition published by Derek Prince Ministries – UK 2017

ISBN 978-1-78263-423-2
Kindle 978-1-78263-306-8
ePub 978-1-78263-305-1
Product code: B117EN3

Unless otherwise indicated, Scripture quotations are
from the *New American Standard Bible*®. Copyright ©
1960, 1962, 1963, 1968, 1971, 1972, 1973 by The
Lockman Foundation.

Scripture identified NIV1984 taken from the Holy Bible,
New International Version®. Copyright © 1973, 1978,
1984 Biblica. Used by permission of Zondervan.

Scripture quotations identified NKJV are from the *New
King James Version*. Copyright © 1982 by Thomas
Nelson, Inc. Used by permission.

This book was compiled from the extensive archives of
Derek Prince's unpublished materials, and edited by
the Derek Prince Ministries editorial team.

Derek Prince Ministries
www.derekprince.com

Contents

Introduction   5

Chapter 1: Christ's Orders   9

Chapter 2: Final Words in Mark   13

Chapter 3: Final Words in Acts   17

Chapter 4: The Process   21

Chapter 5: *The* Sign of Christ's Coming   25

Chapter 6: Receiving the Promises   31

Chapter 7: Miraculous Help   35

Chapter 8: Lessons from Jesus' Pattern   43

Chapter 9: A Unique Obligation   59

Chapter 10: Important Warnings   67

Chapter 11: Preparing to Obey   77

About the Author   82

Books by Derek Prince   84

Derek Prince Ministries Offices Worldwide   86

Introduction

One of the key words utilised in the affairs of any army or military unit is the word *order*. Every soldier is responsible for knowing what is on orders for himself and his unit. Ignorance of orders is not a legitimate excuse for not executing them. A soldier is required to know them.

I have deliberately chosen as the title for this book "Christ's Last Order." As you may know, I am from a military background. Not only were many of my family members in the military, but I also spent five and a half years myself in the British army.

In every army, one of the common slogans you regularly encounter is the following: *ignorance of orders is no excuse*. Once again, a solider is responsible for finding out what the orders are. If you don't know, the fact that you didn't see the noticeboard with the orders on it, or you didn't hear the word of command given is never an excuse.

True for Christians

I believe this same principle is true for us as Christians. If Christ has given us orders, we cannot excuse ourselves by saying, "I never knew about that." God's answer is: *It is all there in the New Testament. You are responsible to acquaint yourself with My orders.*

Another principle in the New Testament (and in the army as well) is that orders remain in force until they are officially cancelled. It doesn't matter whether an order was given five minutes ago or five years ago. It is still in force.

Many Christians seem to have an attitude that says, "Everything written in the New Testament was said such a long while ago. It probably doesn't apply to us today." However, every order Christ gave us is still in force unless it has been cancelled by someone with authority to do it. Frankly, I do not know who that someone would be. Nor do I have any idea of when such a cancellation could have happened.

I believe the orders Christ gave are still in force today. We are responsible for two actions in regard to these orders. First of all, to know them; and second, to do them. Please remember what I said in the beginning: *ignorance of these orders is no excuse for not doing them.*

Chapter 1

Christ's Orders

In this book, the order from Jesus Christ which I am going to highlight is commonly known as the *Great Commission*. You will notice from the theme, however, that I have deliberately changed the word *commission* to *orders*. In my view, the word "commission" doesn't have a sufficiently authoritative sense to it.

Therefore, I want to present the content of this book under the title of "Christ's Orders." They are *not* optional and thus we are not offered any alternatives. These are directives which Jesus requires us to carry out.

All Authority

As the foundation of our study, we will examine three passages in the New Testament. These passages will give us a clear understanding of exactly what Christ's last order is. First, though, it is important to establish by what authority Christ issues these directives.

The mention of authority is revealed in the first of the passages we will cover in Matthew 28:18–20:

Then Jesus came and spoke to them, saying, "All authority has been given to Me in heaven and on earth. Go therefore . . ."

I believe that the word "therefore" is very important. I have often said, "Whenever you find a therefore in the Bible, you want to find out what it's *there for*."

The statement Jesus has just made is connected by the word *therefore* to the order that He goes on to give. To paraphrase, He says, "All authority has been given to Me in heaven and on earth. In the light of that fact, you need to go and exercise that authority by demonstrating it."

You see, authority is completely ineffective unless it is exercised. People may have authority, and never use it at any point in their lives. For them, it would be just as if they never had the authority to begin with.

Here is what Jesus is saying in this verse: *If the world is to know that the authority has been given to Me, you are going to have to demonstrate My authority on My behalf to all nations.* That is how the nations will know that Jesus has the ultimate authority in the world.

Final Words in Matthew

Following this introductory statement, Jesus gives us our orders:

"Go therefore and make disciples of all the nations, baptizing them in the name of the Father and of the Son and of the Holy Spirit, teaching them to observe all things that I have commanded you; and lo, I am with you always, even to the end of the age"

Matthew 28:19–20

What our Lord commands us in that order is a very inclusive statement. Jesus says to go to all the nations. Not one nation anywhere on earth is to be omitted.

Then He says, *"I am with you always, even to the end of the age."* The literal wording of His statement is, "I am with you all the days." If you are familiar with Scandinavian languages, in all the Scandinavian translations it reads "I am with you all the days."

All the days. That is important for us to remember. It is not just a period of time when Jesus will be with us. He will be with us every individual day from now until the close of the age.

We must be careful not to bypass the condition we must fulfil to receive that promise: *obedience*. If we go, He promises to be with us. I *don't* see that He has committed Himself to be with us if we don't go. Our obedience to go is the condition for Him to be with us.

Chapter 2

Final Words in Mark

We see words similar to those in Matthew as we turn to Mark, the next gospel. In the 16th chapter, we see these orders recorded in verses 14–19.

Afterward He appeared to the eleven themselves as they were reclining at the table; and He reproached them for their unbelief and hardness of heart, because they had not believed those who had seen Him after He had risen.

And He said to them, "Go into all the world and preach the gospel to all creation. He who has believed and has been baptized shall be saved; but he who has disbelieved shall be condemned.

"These signs will accompany those who have believed: in My name they will cast out demons, they will speak with new tongues; they will pick up serpents, and

if they drink any deadly poison, it will not hurt them; they will lay hands on the sick, and they will recover."

So then, when the Lord Jesus had spoken to them, He was received up into heaven and sat down at the right hand of God.

In this account in Mark we see that, in a sense, the Lord has done His part. Where in Matthew, Jesus says that all authority has been given to Him, and tells us to go;" Mark says that Jesus ascended into heaven and sat down.

A Finished Work

What does the phrase "He sat down" mean? In the book of Hebrews as well, you will find it emphasised that "He sat down," (see Hebrews 10:11–13). Unlike the liturgical priests who always remain standing, it clearly states that the Messiah sat down.

Why did Jesus sit down? Because His task was complete. The priests remained standing because their task was never complete. So, stating that Jesus sat down is a way of saying His job had been perfectly done. Going forward, the responsibility was on the disciples.

Jesus sat down, but the disciples went and preached everywhere. Again, we notice that the command Jesus gave in Mark is a very all-inclusive order: "Go into all the world." That is very total. "All the world and preach the gospel to every creature." How could anything be more inclusive than that?

Probably you are aware that St Francis of Assisi used to preach to the birds and the animals because he felt they were included in "every creature." Actually, there are many evidences that the birds and animals responded to St Francis in a way they didn't respond to other people.

Personally, I believe they got the message. In a certain sense, I believe we are obligated to the entire created world to present the good news to them. All the world. Every creature.

Proclamation: Not Explanation

Where it says *preach* here in the Mark account, I think we might get a clearer understanding if we translated it as *proclaim*. A proclamation is to be made to the entire world. This has been one of the most satisfying aspects I have experienced in developing my radio programme. I feel I am making a proclamation through the broadcast.

Sometimes we feel we have to explain the whole gospel. Actually, I'm not sure that the gospel can ever be explained completely to human understanding. Rather than explaining it, we have been commanded to proclaim it. Once we obey this order, we can trust the Holy Spirit to do what He will through the proclamation.

There are times when it is more effective not to try and explain everything. When I was first a preacher, having been a philosopher, I felt everything I said needed to be explained. The result was that the explanation became so involved and wearisome that the impact was lost.

Today, many times, I simply rely upon the Holy Spirit. When I proclaim a truth, I trust the Holy Spirit to do what I cannot do. He is the one who will help by way of explanation and application.

Chapter 3

Final Words in Acts

We have examined the final words of Jesus in the gospels of Matthew and Mark. In this chapter, we will examine a third passage. These verses are similar, although the command is expressed slightly differently. The account we will study in this chapter is found in Acts 1:6–8. The incident takes place after the resurrection of Jesus and just before He ascended into heaven.

> [And] *when they had come together, they asked Him, saying, "Lord, will You at this time restore the kingdom to Israel?"*

In the question the disciples ask, I find it interesting that they were still convinced that the time would come when the kingdom would be restored to Israel. In reply, Jesus did not say that it would not happen. However, He did tell them it was not their business to know when it would take place.

And he said to them, "It's not for you to know times or seasons which the Father has put in His own authority. But you shall receive power when the Holy Spirit has come upon you; and you shall be witnesses to Me in Jerusalem, and in all Judea and Samaria, and to the end of the earth."

We read in the following verse what happened next:

[And] *when He had spoken these things, while they watched, He was taken up . . .*

The words Jesus spoke to them in Acts 1:7–8 were apparently the last words that fell from His lips on earth. To me, that is tremendously significant.

Parting Words

For people who are dear to me, the last point I want to make to them is the truth I want them to remember most. I believe that was also true in the relationship of Jesus to His disciples. The last words He spoke were the ones He wanted them to remember most.

What were those words? "To the end of the earth." I believe they descended from the Mount of Olives with that phrase ringing in their minds: "To the end of the earth, to the end of the earth, to the end of the earth." Here is what Jesus was saying to them: "Your task is not complete until you have reached earth's utmost boundaries."

A Composite Picture

If you pull together these three passages we have studied, you get a tremendous accumulation of emphatic words and phrases.

- In Matthew 28 – *"all the nations"* and *"to the end of the age."*

- In Mark 16 – *"all the world"* and *"every creature."*

- And in Acts 1 – *"to the end of the earth."*

Both in time and geography, every extremity is covered. Nothing is omitted or left untouched. It would be impossible, I think, to compile words more clear and more emphatic than these.

If we do not understand and apply these last orders from Jesus Christ, the reason is not because they are not clear. Humbly speaking, I am something of an expert in the interpretation of language. From that position, I would say it would be impossible to say anything more clearly or more emphatically than Jesus has said in these passages.

Chapter 4

The Process

In the preceding chapters, we have clearly seen the orders issued to us by Jesus Christ. They represent His last orders to us which He expects us to obey. In this chapter, we will take a look at the process – how we can fulfil the command given to us by Jesus. Along with Jesus' orders, there are three different kinds of activity implied by the words that are used for communicating the gospel.

In Matthew, Jesus says "make disciples." That is a process of training people.

In Mark He says "proclaim." We may proclaim to millions of people who never become disciples. But even if they don't become disciples, we are still obligated to make the proclamation.

In Acts, Jesus says, "you shall be my witnesses." Witnessing is not preaching. Preaching is proclaiming the truth of God's

Word. However, being a witness is demonstrating the truth by the way you live and by the words you speak.

Being a Witness

Lots of people who are not called to preach can be very effective witnesses. It is so important that we understand the difference between preaching – which I regard as a task not assigned to the whole body – and witnessing, which I believe is to be a responsibility of every Christian.

We commonly use the word witnessing. However, I don't believe it is really the best word, because it suggests something rather religious and almost technical. Let's keep in mind that Jesus said, "You will be my witnesses." His statement would imply that it is actually not necessary to say a lot. In some cases, we inadvertently spoil our witness by talking too much.

To be a witness means that we live in such a way in front of people that there is no other explanation for our lives except that Jesus is alive. That is, I believe, what it truly means to be a witness.

Lydia's Witness

How much speaking we do depends on the leading of the Holy Spirit in any given circumstance. In this regard, I always remember the example of my first wife, Lydia. She met the Lord and was filled with the Holy Spirit while she was a teacher in a government school in Denmark. She became (and always remained) a very bold witness.

She would tell everybody what had happened to her, including people who probably were somewhat insulted by being told. One day she got a new maid to come and look after her house, because as a teacher, she had to attend to responsibilities at the school. For some reason, she never testified of her faith to this maid. For months on end, Lydia did not share anything with her maid concerning her relationship with the Lord.

One day the maid began to cry. In response Lydia asked, "What's the matter with you?" The maid replied, "I know God doesn't love me." Curious about the maid's statement, Lydia enquired, "Why do you think that?" The maid said, "You talk to everybody else about the Lord and you never talk to me. I'm sure God doesn't love me."

Then the maid admitted something to Lydia. She said that before she went to work for Lydia, she had told all her friends, "I know that holy teacher is going to spend all her time telling me about Jesus." In the end, the fact that Lydia didn't tell her about Jesus was what won the lady to the Lord.

So you see, it is always a matter of the leading of the Holy Spirit. It is not a technique. It may be fine to know the four spiritual laws. But you can't get everybody "on the same hook" with "the same bait." To be a witness requires a reliance upon the Holy Spirit.

Chapter 5

The Sign of Christ's Coming

As we consider Christ's last order for us and how to fulfil it, we also need to maintain a sense of the times in which we live. We need to be aware of how long we have to obey this order.

In that regard, let's now consider another passage in Matthew 24. This section of scripture is the great prophetic discourse in which Jesus outlines the sequence of events from His time on earth to the time of His return again in glory.

A Key Question

The discourse in Matthew 24 is triggered by a question asked by some of the disciples of Christ. First we will read the question, and later we will examine the culmination of Jesus' answer. The question is found in verse 3 of Matthew 24:

Now as He sat on the Mount of Olives, the disciples came to Him privately, saying, "Tell us, when will these things be? And what will be the sign of Your coming, and of the end of the age?"

Actually their inquiry to Jesus is a three-fold question:

1. The first part is, "When will all these things happen?" These things being the destruction of the temple.

2. Then the next question is either a single or a double question according to your understanding: "What will be the sign of Your coming?" and,

3. Lastly, "What is the sign of the end of the age?"

In this section, let's deal only with the latter questions the disciples asked: *"What will be **the** sign of Your coming and of the end of the age?"*

In the verses that follow these questions, Jesus gives them a list of signs. He cites international wars, earthquakes, pestilences, famines, false prophets, persecution of Christians, lawlessness and various prophetic pointers like that.

All those are certainly signs. However, they are not *the* sign. Up to that point, Jesus has not specifically answered the precise question, *"What will be the sign of Your coming?"*

This Gospel of the Kingdom

It is not until verse 14 that Jesus gives an answer to the disciples' question. It was a specific question – and He gave a specific answer. It is important for us to see this. Jesus says:

"This gospel of the kingdom will be preached in all the world as a witness to all the nations, and then the end will come."

That is the answer. What will be the sign? The sign will be the preaching of this gospel of the kingdom. Not some watered-down version, but the same gospel Jesus and the early Church preached.

What is the final specific sign of the end of the age? It is the preaching of the gospel of the kingdom in all the world to all nations.

Single-minded

In a sense, we could probably say that Jesus had a one-track mind. He just had one supreme objective clearly before Him: the preaching of the gospel in all the world to all nations. I think sometimes many of us need to be much more single-minded than we are.

We tend to get distracted with a lot of lesser truths or more complicated matters. As a result, the real impact of the important, simple truths may escape us. My desire would be that every person I teach would have a one-track mind like Jesus had.

Let's restate the question once more: "What will be *the sign* of His coming?" The simple yet specific answer is: the preaching of the gospel of the kingdom in all nations in all the world.

What is our responsibility in regard to the return of the Lord? What part do we have to play in bringing it to pass? Here is our answer: the preaching of the gospel of the kingdom in all the world to all nations.

Please note: I am *not* saying that the coming of Jesus depends solely on what we do. But what we do *is* definitely a factor that must be taken into account.

Avoiding Disobedience

In a certain sense, I believe it is possible for the Church to delay the return of the Lord by failing to carry out this responsibility. My understanding is that in God's foreknowledge, there is a specific day and hour appointed for the return of Jesus. However, that return could have taken place earlier had the Church been obedient. In other words, God's foreknowledge takes into account the disobedience of the Church. But it does not exonerate the Church for its disobedience.

Here is what I want to say to you plainly and simply: if we do not follow the instructions clearly outlined to us from the Scriptures, we are disobedient. There is no other accurate word to describe our attitude and our conduct except *disobedience*. In our next chapter, we will cover a helpful point that will further correct our attitude about obeying Christ's orders.

Chapter 6

Receiving the Promises

It's strange, isn't it? When it comes to the promises of Jesus, the Church has no problem in fully embracing them. But when it comes to His orders, we somehow think they are optional or that they simply apply to somebody else!

Basic Promises

In the following section, I want to give a few simple examples of the promises of Jesus. Let's begin in Matthew 21:22:

"And all things, whatever you ask in prayer, believing, you will receive."

In response to such a promise, we readily say, "Praise the Lord" and "Amen" – and that is right. It is certainly a good practice for us to accept such promises and respond positively to them.

Now, let's also look at Mark 11:24:

"Therefore I say to you, whatever things you ask when you pray, believe that you receive them, and you will have them."

Once again, we all say, "Amen." We are glad to accept this wonderful promise.

Next, we turn to another promise in John 14:12–14:

"Most assuredly, I say to you, he who believes in Me, the works that I do he will do also; and greater works than these he will do, because I go to My Father.

And whatever you ask in My name, that I will do, that the Father [might] *be glorified in the Son. If you ask anything in My name, I will do it."*

No problem with these statements. You and I can exclaim, "Praise God. That's a promise for us today!" It hasn't been cancelled. It hasn't gone out of date. It still applies. We can thank God it is still applicable for us today.

Another Promise

Let's consider one more Scripture along the same lines – John 15:7–8.

"If you abide in Me, and My words abide in you, you will ask what you desire, and it shall be done for you. By this My Father is glorified, that you bear much fruit; so you will be My disciples."

You and I can praise the Lord that this is another wonderful promise still valid today.

At this point, however, let me ask a question. Is there any logical basis whatever for thinking that the promises still apply, but the orders have been cancelled? Hopefully, none of us would say, "That is exactly the way I see it." Just like the promises, the orders of Jesus still apply.

Basically, though, the attitude of the Church needs some adjustment. Most of us gladly embrace the promises. But sometimes, we are not as concerned as we need to be about carrying out the orders. I believe that is inconsistent.

In our next chapter, we will address that inconsistency – and receive some encouragement about handling the task before us.

Chapter 7

Miraculous Help

From what we have examined up to this point, we know that Christ's last order to us is to present the gospel to the entire world. We might tend to regard this as an overwhelming assignment. In that regard, let me illustrate the task Jesus has set before us from a specific series of miracles that took place in His ministry.

An Immense Task

Let's begin by freely admitting that the thought of reaching the entire world might discourage us and keep us from obedience. When we consider what is involved in preaching the gospel to a world that has a population of seven billion or more people, that task seems so immense. Where do we begin? Who can face a challenge like that?

It is possible for us to feel that the task is so immense we could never carry it through. It is possible for us to allow ourselves to be discouraged from even beginning – which is illogical and inexcusable. Truthfully, I think this might be the psychological attitude of many Christians.

True, the world is vast. There are so many different nations and so many different languages and so many different cultures. How could we ever really do what Jesus told us to do?

When we look at the task before us from that point of view, we recognise another troubling fact. The job isn't getting any easier – because the population of the world is increasing. In many ways, the complexity of cultures and languages is increasing at the same rate as the population increase.

Feeding the Multitudes

In the face of these stark realities, I want to offer what I believe is a pattern for how Jesus intended us to go about this task. Primarily, I want to approach it from the perspective of the miracle of the feeding of the five thousand.

Along with that incident, I want to include the subsequent miracle of the feeding of the four thousand. To help us see the application, I will later add a lesson which Jesus Himself pointed out in regard to these two miracles.

In some ways, the miracle of the feeding of the five thousand is a very unique miracle. It is the only supernatural incident that is recorded in all four gospels. There is not another miracle that Jesus performed during His earthly ministry which is recorded in all four gospels. In addition, it is the only miracle which Jesus Himself commented on. He had a specific application for it.

Let's examine the account of the feeding of the five thousand as it is recorded in Matthew 14:13–21.

When Jesus heard it [about John the Baptist's beheading], *He departed from there by boat to a deserted place by Himself. But when the multitudes heard it, they followed Him on foot from the cities. And when Jesus went out He saw a great multitude; and He was moved with compassion for them, and healed their sick.*

When it was evening, His disciples came to Him, saying, "This is a deserted place, and the hour is already late. Send the multitudes away, that they may go into the villages and buy themselves food."

But Jesus said to them, "They do not need to go away. You give them something to eat." They said to Him, "We have here only five loaves and two fish." He said, "Bring them here to Me."

Then He commanded the multitudes to sit down on the grass. And He took the five loaves and the two fish, and looking to heaven, He blessed and broke and gave the loaves to the disciples; and the disciples gave to the multitudes.

So they all ate and were filled, and they took up twelve baskets full of the fragments that remained. Now those who had eaten were about five thousand men, besides women and children.

In regard to the actual number of people involved, I would imagine the number of women and children probably equalled the number of men. We don't know exactly, but if that is the case, it would mean ten thousand persons in all were miraculously fed.

Another Miraculous Feeding

Let's immediately move on now to the next example where we have a similar miracle. In this case, however, the figures are different.

The account of the feeding of the four thousand is recorded in Matthew 15:32–39.

Then Jesus called His disciples to Him and said, "I have compassion on the multitude, because they have now continued with Me three days, and have nothing to eat. And I do not want to send them away hungry, lest they faint on the way."

Then His disciples said to Him, "Where could we get enough bread in the wilderness to fill such a great multitude?" Jesus said to them, "How many loaves do you have?" And they said, "Seven, and a few little fish."

And He commanded the multitude to sit down on the ground. And He took the seven loaves and the fish and gave thanks, broke them and gave them to His disciples; and the disciples gave to the multitude.

So they all ate and were filled, and they took up seven large baskets full of the fragments that were left. Now those who ate were four thousand men, besides women and children. And He sent away the multitude, got into the boat, and came to the region of Magdala.

Next, the disciples crossed the lake with Jesus. Somewhere in the process, they realised they had forgotten to take bread with them. It is in this context that Jesus comments on the two miracles of the feeding of the five thousand and the four thousand.

Specific Numbers

In the verses which follow, I want you to notice that Jesus is very specific about all the figures involved. He expected His disciples to remember and learn from the numbers pertaining to these two miracles. We see this beginning in Matthew 16:5–11:

And when His disciples had come to the other side [of the lake], *they had forgotten to take bread. Then Jesus said to them, "Take heed and beware of the leaven of the Pharisees and the Sadducees."*

And they reasoned among themselves [quite wrongly], *saying, "It is because we have taken no bread." When Jesus perceived it, He said to them, "O you of little faith, why do you reason among yourselves because you have brought no bread?*

Do you not yet understand, or remember the five loaves of the five thousand and how many baskets you took up? [Nor] *the seven loaves of the four thousand, and how many large baskets you took up? How is it you do not understand . . . ?"*

Please note that Jesus recapitulated for them all the essential figures of each of those miracles – the five thousand and the four thousand.

What are the implications of Jesus' discourse with them about the number of people who had been fed? This will be the focus of our next chapter.

Chapter 8

Lessons from Jesus' Pattern

We have looked at the accounts of the feeding of the five thousand and the feeding of the four thousand. Then, we have seen that Jesus referred specifically to these numbers to make a point to His disciples. What can we glean from all this? Very simply, I want to take the challenge of feeding a multitude of say ten thousand or eight thousand people with virtually no food as a pattern for us. In essence, it is an example to us of the challenge of presenting the gospel to a world of seven billion people.

In this chapter, I want to extract principles from the feeding of these multitudes which I believe apply exactly to the task of presenting the gospel to the entire world.

An Impossible Task?

Clearly, we have to acknowledge that what Jesus asked the disciples to do was *totally impossible*. They had no natural ability or means to do what He required of them. Yet, He required them to do it.

In mathematical terms, if I were to compare the impossibility of feeding ten thousand persons with five loaves and two fishes with the impossibility of presenting the gospel to the whole world today, I would have to say the first is the greater of the two impossibilities. It is totally impossible.

Whereas, in light of the world situation today with modern means of communication and travel, along with the resources available to the Church, it is not exactly impossible to present the gospel to the whole world. But it is certainly an immense task.

In this chapter, I want to take these two comparisons and apply some very simple lessons for our benefit. These lessons will relate to our task of presenting the gospel to the entire world – to every nation, to every creature, to the ends of the earth. From these two accounts of miraculous supply, I want to extract five simple lessons or principles.

1. Don't Avoid the Responsibility

First of all, when we read the account of the feeding of the five thousand in Matthew's gospel, it is very clear that the disciples did not want the responsibility of feeding five thousand people.

They said, "It's getting late. Send them away now so they still have time to go somewhere to get food before it gets dark." The disciples had enough sense to see this was going to be a major problem. Their attitude was: "Let's avoid it." To a large degree, the attitude of the Church today is commonly the same.

However, let's take note of how Jesus regarded that responsibility. This is what Jesus said to His disciples: "**You** give them something to eat." I believe this same principle is exactly true for the Church today. We may also want to escape the responsibility of presenting the gospel to the whole world. But Jesus says in effect, "It is your job. It is your responsibility. I have ordered you to do it. And I have never retracted the order."

2. Use the Natural and the Supernatural

Second, there are two essential components I want to point out as illustrations from the feeding of the five thousand and the four thousand. Those miracles point to a very important relationship between two concepts, which tend to be regarded by some Christians as almost opposites.

Let me say in general, Christians tend to be very simplistic in their approach. When confronted with two statements which are different, Christians often assume they have to make a choice for one over the other. For instance, some Christians make a distinction and choice between the gifts of the Spirit and the fruit of the Spirit. But they are not alternatives.

God doesn't say, "I'm so impoverished that if I give you gifts I can't afford to let you have fruit." God says, "I expect you to have fruit and exercise it through the gifts." The gifts are the means to make fruit available. They are not contrary to fruit. The two complement one another.

In this situation of the feeding of the multitudes, I see again two aspects which are often regarded as inconsistent with one another. And yet, they are not. The one is what I would call *order* or *discipline*. The other is *God's supernatural power*.

Some church groups tend to focus on one or the other. There is the order/discipline group. Everybody lined up; everybody with their own leader; everybody accountable; everybody doing exactly what they are supposed to be doing; everybody in their proper place.

Now, that is not wrong. In fact, it is very clearly demonstrated in the feeding of the five thousand.

> *Jesus said, "Make them sit down in groups of fifty."*
>
> Luke 9:14b

If He hadn't done that, some of the people would never have been fed. The people at the front may have taken more than their share, and the people at the back would have never received anything. Believe me, that is human nature when people are hungry. If you have seen starving people, you know they can lose their manners very quickly. Possibly, there might have been some people trampled under foot. Some may even have lost their lives in the rush of the multitude to receive this food.

So, it was imperative that the disciples begin with order – getting everybody into a reasonably sized group that could be dealt with. To me, that is a very clear example of the importance of order, of authority and of discipleship.

Let me point out here, however, that they could have gotten everybody neatly ordered in groups of fifty and left them hungry! What good would that have been? Order by itself was not sufficient. It was necessary, but not sufficient. To make that order effective, the supernatural grace and power of God had to be released.

Supernatural power in the service of the Lord is not an option. It is a necessity. It is not something you can have if you choose. "Well, he's the kind of person who goes after those kinds of things. I'm not much interested in that. I just want to lead a quiet, decent, orderly Christian life. Miracles and gifts of the Spirit are all well and good. But I'm not that kind of person."

I don't believe any of us has a right to take that attitude. In fact, I believe it is unscriptural. As Bob Mumford has said, "The gifts of the Spirit are not toys, they're tools." They have to be there to get the job done.

Here is what I want to suggest as the second principle for us. To work a miracle, order and discipline have to be *balanced* and *complemented* by the supernatural power of God.

In this second principle, I am not just thinking in terms of miracles of healing or provision. I am talking about a miraculous way of looking at our lives as a whole. We need a miraculous approach to life – an approach that never says, "I'm limited to my own ability and my own resources." Instead it is an approach to life which views every situation in the light of God's unlimited resources. That is what I mean by a supernatural approach to life.

3. Share the Blessing

The third principle from the miracle of feeding the multitudes is that the multiplication did not depend merely on Jesus. Rather, it depended on the disciples passing on what they received from Jesus. If the disciples had not passed on what they had received, the miracle would never have been consummated.

Once again, I believe the same is true with you and me in regard to the grace of God. It is not dependent only on Jesus. It originates with

Jesus – but it has to be completed by our cooperation and activity.

This is the point we need to see in the task of reaching the entire world. The grace originates with Jesus. The power originates with Jesus. The provision originates with Jesus. But for the world to receive it, we have to receive it and pass it on. In that regard, we can either become *channels* or *barriers*.

Channels or barriers. I am inclined to think those are the only options we have. There isn't any other alternative. When God gives an order and makes His grace available, we have just two options. You and I can become either a channel of it or a barrier to it.

Here is what I would like to suggest to you as you read this book: you are either a channel or a barrier. Frankly, if you're not a channel, you are a barrier. There are no grey areas. You either go forward in faith or you go back into unbelief. There are no other choices.

In these times, I see many Christians backsliding – not because they wanted to sin, but because they were afraid to go forward in faith. That is perhaps one of the greatest dangers which confronts us as Christians – being afraid to move forward in faith. Instead, we want to play it safe. We want to be secure. We don't want to take the risk. We want to just sit where we are and be nice.

I don't believe we have the option to do any of what I have just listed. We cannot have it that way. I believe we either go forward into more faith or we go back into unbelief. The sobering result of going back, according to the writer of Hebrews, is that unbelief leads to perdition or eternal damnation.

Concerning the people who choose unbelief over faith, God says,

"My soul has no pleasure in him."

Hebrews 10:38b)

For us, the options are not complicated. They are very clear.

4. Step into Abundance

The fourth principle I see in the miracle of these feedings is that multiplication continued until all the needs were met – and beyond. Clearly, everybody was fed. But beyond that, after everybody was fed, they had a lot more left over. There was more at the end than at the beginning. That is no accident.

In these miracles, I believe Jesus is demonstrating that God's resources are limitless. He is never limited to just meeting the need. He always has abundance.

Abundance is one of the key words in understanding God. In fact, I don't know any one word which better describes God than the word abundance.

God always has more than enough. As I understand Scripture, He is always willing to make available to us more than enough.

We see this truth clearly in 2 Corinthians 9:8:

God is able to make all grace abound toward [us], *that* [we], *always having all sufficiency in all things, may abound to every good work.*

Sufficiency is having enough. Abundance is having more than enough. But the abundance that is given to us is *not* for selfish pleasure and indulgence. It is for "every good work."

5. Experience a Greater Surplus

The final point I want to extract from these miracles is this: the greater the need and the fewer the resources, the greater the surplus you will experience. That statement is really almost comical, so I want to say it again: *The greater the need and the fewer the resources, the greater the surplus.*

Let's go back now to the accounts of the miracles so we can see the exact figures:

In the first miracle, there were five thousand men; in the second there were only four thousand. In the first miracle, they had five loaves and two fishes. In the second, they had seven loaves and a few little fishes.

Here are the statistics, in the first miracle the number of people to be fed was larger, yet the resources with which they started were smaller.

You will remember that when Jesus was reminding His disciples of these miracles in Matthew 14 and 16, He was very insistent that they remember what was left over. In fact, here is an interesting note. When you read the account in all four gospels, you discover it was Jesus' idea to pick up the fragments. Our Lord has always been a member of the anti-litter league!

The disciples, very possibly, would have walked away and left the place littered. But

Jesus said, "Gather up the fragments that remain, so that nothing is lost" (John 6:12).

In the first miracle, they had twelve large baskets of fragments. In the second miracle, they had seven picnic baskets of the fragments. It is difficult to be absolutely sure, but I have looked these words up in the most reliable Greek dictionaries. It appears that the baskets in the first miracle were larger than the baskets in the second.

At the end of the first miracle, they gathered up twelve larger baskets. At the end of the second miracle, they gathered up seven smaller baskets. Jesus told them to remember the numbers – what they started with, how many were fed, and what was left-over.

Why was He so insistent? I am sure He was emphasising this fifth principle from these miracles. Let's state it once again: *The greater the need and the fewer the resources, the greater the surplus.* God will always make sure we realise that there is no shortage with Him.

The bigger the challenge, the less we have to start with, the more we can expect God's abundance. That is where you and I have to change our thinking.

Every one of us is a slave of our thinking. Rarely are we able to move beyond the way we envisage life as we know it. But believing the Bible means a revolution for all of us in our way of thinking.

A Personal Test

By way of personal testimony, I was once confronted with a decision about the future course of my own ministry. I received a proposal – a very intelligent and sensible one – as to how I could expand and increase my ministry.

In retrospect, I think the proposal I received represented a God-ordained choice I had to make. As I meditated on the proposed plan to increase my ministry, I saw that if I were to accept it, I would be going against certain basic principles God had specifically taught me over the years.

Eventually I made my decision. I said, "Lord, I'm going to trust You for the increase. I'm not going to use perfectly legitimate but somewhat carnal methods. If You are not the source of the increase, I'm really not too interested in it happening."

As I look back on the choice I made, I appreciate being confronted with this decision. Why? Because it tested me and required me to make a statement about where I put my trust. From the moment I made that decision, I have felt a release in my own spirit.

Without going into further details, the suggested way of increasing the ministry was perfectly legitimate. In fact, it is the method followed by many ministries in this country. But when I considered it for myself, I saw that it wasn't the way the Lord had led me or wanted me to go.

At the core of my decision was a basic desire to reach out more. Rather than spend more time building my own base or catering to my own financial needs, I decided to spend more time reaching out to people who are not yet reached. Rather than securing my financial base, I decided to reach out in a greater way to those for whom much of the Church doesn't care at all.

That decision did not mean that I was not interested in financial security. Rather it meant that I could reach a larger crowd with smaller resources, and still expect a greater surplus. That's the way I saw it then – and that's the way I see it now.

A Quick Recap

To end this chapter, let's have a quick recap of the five principles we can glean from these miraculous feedings of the multitudes.

1. **Don't avoid the responsibility**. It's our job to present the gospel to the whole world.

2. **Use the natural and the supernatural**. It's not either order or supernatural miracles – but the powerful combination of both.

3. **Share the blessing**. Jesus is the source, but He expects us to be channels – not barriers – of His blessing.

4. **Step into abundance**. God not only meets the need; He pours out more than is needed.

5. **Experience a greater surplus**. The greater the need and the fewer the resources, the greater the surplus.

Let's move on now to our next chapter, in which we will discover how to apply these valuable principles.

Chapter 9

A Unique Obligation

At this point in your reading of this book, my desire is to help you apply the principles I have been seeking to unfold. Let me repeat what I said early in this book. In the light of what I have presented to you from the New Testament, I believe we only have two options: to obey or to disobey. It is a truth that you and I cannot escape – we must obey or disobey.

This statement is not only true for you and me – but also for God's people in every nation and every land. The whole Church shares this responsibility to present the gospel in every land and nation in which it has not yet been presented.

The discussion which follows applies primarily to the United States and to other Western nations. In a very real sense, however, it should prompt questions in every Christian. Questions like: "What about me? What do I have that I can share? What about the gifts

I have beyond material wealth? How can I best use them for the benefit of the whole Church?"

Even though I will be speaking primarily about financial resources, we need to realise that spiritual resources are fundamental to the building of the kingdom. If we have spiritual gifts, how can we best utilise them?

Great Resources/ Great Responsibility

I believe there is a certain principle which Jesus unfolds in the New Testament which makes the responsibility of Christians in the United States greater than that of almost any other group of Christians. This principle is stated in the latter part of Luke 12:48:

"For everyone to whom much is given, from him much will be required; and to whom much has been committed, of him they will ask the more."

What Jesus is saying here is extremely clear and very logical. The more you possess, and the more you have available to you, the more God will require from you. It is a simple matter of proportion.

A Matter of Perspective

Financially, the United States is one of the wealthiest, most powerful nations in the world. There are other nations today which might possibly have a higher standard of living. Switzerland is one, Norway is another. But there are very few which exceed the sheer wealth of the United States.

Even those who are living below what is called "the poverty level" in the United States are better off than most of the world. Even the poor in America – compared with the world at large – are relatively wealthy.

I wish I could communicate this truth more effectively. I think that many American Christians have very little concept of how the rest of the world lives – how the Third World lives, how Asia lives, how Africa lives, how South America lives.

Certainly, there is genuine poverty in the United States. Yet, even the poorest in the U.S. usually have a choice of what they can eat, slim though it may be. I would say more than half the world has no choice, and over seven and a half million people are probably going to die of starvation this year.

Many of us are used to having sheets on our beds. Most of the world has never seen a sheet and wouldn't know what to do with one. Many of us expect to wear shoes on our feet. I question whether half the world wears shoes on its feet. You and I would have a hard time imagining what it would be like to have never worn a pair of shoes.

Even when I was in Kenya many decades ago – and Kenya is a relatively well-to-do Third World country – I can remember the delight my students experienced when, for the first time, they put a pair of shoes on their feet.

The Bible says in the Song of Solomon (7:1), "How beautiful are thy feet with shoes, O prince's daughter." I once heard someone say that you really feel like a prince's daughter when you get shoes on your feet. You wouldn't understand that statement unless you had faced a situation where you didn't have shoes.

Possibly some from an older generation knew what it was to take off their shoes to walk to school. I have known people who couldn't afford to wear out their shoes. So they would carry their shoes to school so as not to wear them out, and then put them on when they got to school. Few of us, however, have had that experience.

The main point of all this discussion is that what we consider poor, a majority of the world would consider wealthy.

Freedom of Religion

The wealth enjoyed in the United States is one clear distinctive. Not merely that, but the liberty enjoyed by American Christians is significant as well. The freedom available to practise religion with protection – even with special favours and provisions from the government – is somewhat unique.

There may not be any other country in the world where Christians have the same privileges such as tax exemption for churches, for example. I doubt whether there is another nation on earth which might even think of such a concept. Most other nations today – even nominally Christian nations – would try to extract services from the Church, not make them available to the Church.

Once again, my point is that those who live in the United States have unique privileges and unique opportunities unrivalled anywhere else on earth.

Abundant Materials

Consider one other unique privilege of English-speaking Christians, whatever their colour or race. There is teaching material available in English on a scale that is not available in any other language or any other nation.

I'm speaking specifically here about practical Bible teaching that tells a person how to apply the Bible to one's life – what the Word of God means in plain speech rather in abstract, remote, or theological terms. My guess would be – and it is simply a guess – that 90 per cent of all such material is in English.

Even in civilised, intellectual, educated nations like Germany, it is very hard to find that kind of literature in the German language. In French it is almost non-existent. Perhaps Sweden would be the country that comes nearest, but it is far, far behind the English-speaking countries. In all of this, we need to be mindful of the Scripture that says,

> *"To whom much is given, from him also shall much be required."*
>
> Luke 12:48

We are uniquely privileged. I believe I can say that because I am an American citizen by naturalisation. I was educated and brought up in Britain. Britain is certainly a privileged nation, but Christians in Britain are not half as privileged as Christians in the United States.

What does all this mean? It means that we in the United States – because of the abundance of our resources – carry a greater share of the responsibility for communicating the gospel to all nations. Much has been given to us and we thank God for it. But much more is required from us.

This isn't a reason to despair and feel condemned. Rather, it should be a motivation to recognise what we have and then ask for God's wisdom and direction on how to invest it most effectively in His kingdom.

Chapter 10

Important Warnings

As we draw near to the end of this book, I want to provide what I would call "relevant warnings." As always, it is my intention that this message be extremely practical. I do not want just to stir your emotions.

If stirring your emotions was all this book could achieve, I wouldn't even try to communicate these truths. Why? Because if your emotions merely are stirred and your will is not affected, you will be under greater condemnation from now on than you were before. Putting you under condemnation is clearly not my intention. So let me offer at this point just a few relevant warnings.

1. Begin to Change Your Attitude

First, try to discern whether change is needed in any area of your life. The purpose of what has been presented thus far in this book is to lead you to determine whether your life is fully lined up with the orders Jesus has given. But if any change is required, primarily it should be a change of attitude, not action.

I am not suggesting that in the next thirty minutes you have to do something totally different from what you have been doing. What I do believe is that most of us need a change of attitude. That is primary. If I can help you begin that process through this book, I will be very satisfied.

2. Decide if You Should Go or Stay

The second principle is to make a decision about how and when you should serve. It should be obvious to you and me that all of us should not or could not "go." In fact, it would be chaotic if we all did.

As to who should actually "go" and who should "stay," that is something the Holy Spirit has to indicate to us individually and collectively. What I am giving you is general direction which comes from Scripture. *Particular direction comes from the Holy Spirit individually.*

However, please bear this in mind. Even if you do not go, you should see yourself just as totally involved as those who do go. I would like you to think this way: "I will regard whoever has gone or will go as my brother, my sister, my child." You should view those who "go" in exactly this way.

They should be as close to you and as important to you as the closest members of your family. Everything that happens to them – good or bad – should be of concern to you, if you have the right attitude.

3. Discern Your God-Given Sphere

Third, each individual and each fellowship must discern their God-given sphere. Each of us has a God-given sphere as individuals. I believe the same is true for groups of believers. In applying this teaching on Christ's last order, we have to hear from God as to "What is my individual sphere?" Equally, we have to address the corporate aspect: "What is our collective sphere as a church, ministry, family or community?"

Let me provide two brief examples of this principle from the New Testament. The first is from Galatians 2:7, 9. This passage speaks about a confrontation relating to differing spheres. On one side were Paul and his co-workers. On the other side were Peter, James and John and their co-workers.

> *But on the contrary, when they* [that is, Peter, James and John] *saw that the gospel for the uncircumcised had been committed to me, as the gospel for the circumcised was to Peter . . . and when James, Cephas, and John, who seemed to be pillars, perceived the grace that had been given to me, they gave me and Barnabas the right hand of fellowship, that we should go to the Gentiles, and they to the circumcised.*

Evidently, from the decision described in this passage, there was a very clear demarcation of spheres of responsibility. Interestingly enough, in those days of the early Church, the primary and most important sphere of influence was not the millions of Gentiles – but the little handful of Jews. They were first on the list.

Focusing on the main point of this section, let's recognise the principle of discerning our God-given sphere. In this case, for Peter, James and John, their sphere was the Jewish people:

the circumcised. For Paul and his co-workers, their sphere was the uncircumcised: the Gentile world. They saw the situation clearly and acknowledged that each group had their God-given sphere.

Our second scriptural example concerning sphere is found in 2 Corinthians 10:14. This is just one short verse that may not be worded the same in all translations. But the principle is the same in every rendition of the passage.

> *For we are not extending ourselves beyond our sphere* [thus not reaching you]*, for it was to you that we* [first] *came with the gospel of Christ . . .*

This verse is a complicated sentence in Greek, and there are different ways of translating it. But if you look at various translations, they all boil down to the same truth – that Paul and his co-workers had a specific sphere of responsibility in the total world for which they had to be answerable.

When we consider the task of bringing the gospel to the whole world, we have to acknowledge that it is *our* assignment. It is not somebody else's job. Collectively, it is our task. But within the total task, God allots to each individual and to each group that is organically joined in Him specific spheres of responsibility.

Thinking back to a particular congregation in which I served in the United States, I would say that our primary sphere of responsibility was the same as Peter, James and John. It was to the Jews. While the sphere of our church was not limited to the Jewish people in our area, I believe they were our number one priority.

God had revealed that to us, and we accepted the assignment. Nobody planned it or anticipated it. However, I would say that we, as a particular congregation, had a greater impact on the Jewish community in our geographical area than all the surrounding churches put together. It is not something to boast about. Rather, it is something to operate in as an expression of "being in our sphere."

Lydia, my first wife, was called specifically to the Jewish people in Palestine. Privately she would say to me, "If you observe the people who are called to the Jews, they are different from the ones who are called to the Gentiles. Those called to the Jews are usually older and more mature."

In contrast, I often saw God send young people to Africa and to China. In a way, they didn't have to have a lot of worldly wisdom. If those same young people had been sent to the Jewish community, they probably would not have been well received. It is a matter of operating in your God-given sphere.

The principle I am highlighting here is this: you must find your sphere. You can cause more harm than good if you thrash around in somebody else's sphere. Additionally, if you fail to carry out your responsibility in your own sphere, you are going to have to answer to God. You have to discern your God-given sphere.

4. Welcome Other Spheres in the Body

Here is the final principle I want to make in this section. Even when others go to a different sphere than ours, we should still see them as our representatives and our responsibility. We cannot allow ourselves to be so small-minded as to not receive and thank God for ministries working in other spheres than our own.

I firmly believe that the gospel needs to be presented to every tribe, nation, language and people. Why? Because there has to be at least one representative from every one of these groups among the redeemed. Revelation 5 verse

9 confirms that every single tribe, nation and tongue will be represented. The Church will not be complete until they are.

That is why I have a tremendous admiration for the work of the Wycliffe Bible translators. Every time I hear about their work, my heart leaps. The work they do is a difficult, unromantic, unrewarding, tough assignment, and they are people of real commitment and dedication.

Personally, I don't believe I am called in any way to do that kind of work. That being said, my attitude is not: 'Well, those people are Wycliffe translators, so they don't have anything to do with me.' Quite to the contrary, I feel they are my representatives. They are doing what I am not able to do – what I am not called to do.

But every time they succeed, I will bless the Lord for them. I will pray for them when it is laid on my heart to pray for them. I will give an offering to their organisation if God prompts me to do so. I am proud of them and the work they do. Clearly, they are working in a different sphere. But they are part of the same Body. And, oh, what we miss if we become small-minded and parochial about these matters.

Principles to Remember

To close out this chapter, let's reiterate the principles we have discovered in it so we can walk in them more effectively.

1. **Begin to change your attitude**. Allow God to show you where you need to line up more fully with the Master's orders.

2. **Decide if you should go or stay**. Regardless of which calling is yours, determine in your heart to support your brothers and sisters in their calling.

3. **Discern your God-given sphere**. Find your assignment and operate effectively in it.

4. **Welcome other spheres in the Body**. Open up your mind and heart to others who are serving in a sphere different from yours.

With these principles clear in our mind – especially the last one of accepting others who have a different calling – let's move to our final chapter of this book. My hope is that it will inspire you in a greater way to obey Christ's last order.

Chapter 11

Preparing to Obey

To close this book, I want to begin our final chapter with an observation about people who are particularly effective in their Christian walk.

As you may know, I travel a lot, meeting a lot of different people. I enjoy this aspect of my work, and consider meeting so many people to be one of the great privileges and blessings of my life. Thankfully, my experience of fellowship is not restricted to one view of Christianity, to one type of Christian or to one kind of Christian group. I meet them all and I love them all. However, I meet some people who are what I would call "high on Christianity." I think you probably know what I mean by that expression.

There is something exhilarating about meeting Christians who are high on Christianity. In fact, I believe we need more people like them. Even though at times, they might do something that embarrasses me a little, I still praise God for them.

I will tell you the two distinctive features I have noticed with these people. Number one, they believe it is their responsibility to reach the whole world with the gospel – a task they take very seriously. Number two, they believe Jesus is coming soon.

Truthfully, I want those two features to be alive in me as well. I don't think I am ever going to be too high on those two convictions. What about you?

Making Ourselves Ready

Throughout this book, we have been considering our response to Christ's last order. The first step is accepting the fact that it is *our* responsibility to reach *all* nations with the gospel of the kingdom. I hope that as I have unfolded this message, you have come to see that Christ's last order is still in force. It is just as pertinent to you and me today as when He first issued it.

As we accept our responsibility for the task of reaching the nations, we recognise the need to begin changing some of our attitudes. We also began to listen to what God is saying individually about our God-given spheres and how He wants us to operate in them – all the while appreciating those who serve in other spheres.

In this final chapter, we have seen another needed component – an awareness of the return of Jesus Christ. This awareness gives us a sense of urgency. Jesus is coming soon, and we as His body, the Church, need to complete the task which He has given us.

As we saw from our study of Matthew 24:14, there is one "sign" that must be fulfilled:

"This gospel of the kingdom will be preached in all the world as a witness to all the nations, and then the end will come."

Our awareness of Jesus' return brings with it a tremendous responsibility – to preach the good news of the kingdom to every tribe, tongue, people and nation.

Taking Some Steps

All too often, when God challenges us with a truth from His Word, we fail to apply it in our lives. Let's make sure, as we conclude this teaching, that we take steps to respond to the challenge God is offering us. Let's respond appropriately to His call to obey Christ's last order.

You may want to take some time to wait on the Lord, listening to His voice for the next step. As I said before, I am not suggesting that in the next thirty minutes you have got to do something totally different from what you have been doing.

A good place to start is always to consider changing some of our attitudes – softening our hearts before God and seeking His higher ways for our life and service to Him.

Also, I invite you to express a prayer of renewed commitment to the Lord. I will lead you in this prayer – though it is not intended to be the end, but the beginning of a new and exciting season of your life in Christ. Please join me in the following prayer.

Heavenly Father, Your Word is so clear concerning the need for every disciple of Jesus to proclaim the gospel of Your kingdom to "all the nations," "to the end of the age," to "all the world" and "every creature," and "to the end of the earth."

Help me to grow in my understanding of the need to share this most precious truth

You have given – the good news of Your kingdom. Please reveal the sphere to which You have called me, and give me Your heart for that sphere, along with the wisdom and discernment to be most effective for You.

I recognize that I have something to give – finances, gifts, skills and abilities You have given to me for Your glory. I lay them before You and ask that You would use them for Your sake. Help me to work together with other Christians, supporting and encouraging my brothers and sisters in the work they are doing for You.

I echo the words of Revelation 22:17, "the Spirit and the bride say, "Come!" And let him who hears say, "Come!" And let him who thirsts come. Whoever desires, let him take the water of life freely." Empower me by Your Holy Spirit that I may help to prepare the way of the Lord.

He who testifies to these things says, "Surely I am coming quickly."

Amen. Even so, come, Lord Jesus!

The grace of our Lord Jesus Christ be with you all. Amen.

About the Author

Derek Prince (1915–2003) was born in India of British parents. Educated as a scholar of Greek and Latin at Eton College and Cambridge University, England, he held a Fellowship in Ancient and Modern Philosophy at King's College. He also studied several modern languages, including Hebrew and Aramaic, at Cambridge University and the Hebrew University in Jerusalem.

While serving with the British army in World War II, he began to study the Bible and experienced a life-changing encounter with Jesus Christ. Out of this encounter he formed two conclusions: first, that Jesus Christ is alive; second, that the Bible is a true, relevant, up-to-date book. These conclusions altered the whole course of his life, which he then devoted to studying and teaching the Bible.

Derek's main gift of explaining the Bible and its teaching in a clear and simple way has helped build a foundation of faith in millions of lives. His non-denominational, non-sectarian approach "Keys to Successful Living" has made his teaching equally relevant and helpful to people from all racial and religious backgrounds.

He is the author of over 50 books, 600 audio and 100 video teachings, many of which have been translated and published in more than 100 languages. His daily radio broadcast is translated into Arabic, Chinese (Amoy, Cantonese, Mandarin, Shanghainese, Swatow), Croatian, German, Malagasy, Mongolian, Russian, Samoan, Spanish and Tongan. The radio programme continues to touch lives around the world.

Derek Prince Ministries continues to reach out to believers in over 140 countries with Derek's teachings, fulfilling the mandate to keep on "until Jesus returns." This is effected through the outreaches of more than 30 Derek Prince Offices around the world, including primary work in Australia, Canada, China, France, Germany, the Netherlands, New Zealand, Norway, Russia, South Africa, Switzerland, the United Kingdom and the United States. For current information about these and other worldwide locations, visit www.derekprince.com

Books by Derek Prince

Appointment in Jerusalem
At the End of Time*
Authority and Power of
    God's Word*
Be Perfect
Blessing or Curse: You
    Can Choose
Bought with Blood
By Grace Alone
Called to Conquer
Choice of a Partner, The
Complete Salvation
Declaring God's Word
Derek Prince – A Biography
    by Stephen Mansfield
Derek Prince: On Experiencing
    God's Power
Destiny of Israel and The
    Church, The
Divine Exchange, The
Doctrine of Baptisms, The*
Does Your Tongue Need
    Healing?
End of Life's Journey, The
Entering the Presence of God
Expelling Demons
Explaining Blessings and
    Curses
Extravagant Love
Faith and Works*
Faith to Live By
Fasting
Final Judgment*

First Mile, The
Foundational Truths for
    Christian Living
Founded on the Rock*
Gifts of the Spirit, The
God is a Matchmaker
God's Medicine Bottle
God's Plan for Your Money
God's Remedy for Rejection
God's Will for Your Life
God's Word Heals
Grace of Yielding, The
Harvest Just Ahead, The
Holy Spirit in You, The
How to Fast Successfully
Husbands and Fathers
Immersion in The Spirit*
Judging
Key to the Middle East, The
Keys to Successful Living
Laying the Foundations
    Series*
Life's Bitter Pool
Life Changing Spiritual
    Power
Living as Salt and Light
Lucifer Exposed
Marriage Covenant, The
Orphans, Widows, the Poor
    and Oppressed
Our Debt to Israel
Pages from My Life's Book
Partners for Life

Philosophy, the Bible and
    the Supernatural
Power in the Name
Power of the Sacrifice, The
Prayers and Proclamations
Praying for the Government
Promise of Provision, The
Prophetic Guide to the
    End Times
Protection from Deception
Pulling Down Strongholds
Receiving God's Best
Rediscovering God's Church
Resurrection of the Body*
Rules of Engagement
Secrets of a Prayer Warrior
Self-Study Bible Course
    (revised and expanded)
Set Apart for God
Shaping History Through
    Prayer and Fasting

Spiritual Warfare
Surviving the Last Days
Thanksgiving, Praise
    and Worship
They Shall Expel Demons
Three Most Powerful
    Words, The
Through Repentance to Faith*
Through the Psalms with
    Derek Prince
Transmitting God's Power*
Three Messages for Israel
Two Harvests, The
War in Heaven
Where Wisdom Begins
Who is the Holy Spirit?
Will You Intercede?
You Matter to God
You Shall Receive Power

Get the Complete Laying the Foundations Series*

1. Founded on the Rock (B100)
2. Authority and Power of God's Word (B101)
3. Through Repentance to Faith (B102)
4. Faith and Works (B103)
5. The Doctrine of Baptisms (B104)
6. Immersion in The Spirit (B105)
7. Transmitting God's Power (B106)
8. At the End of Time (B107)
9. Resurrection of the Body (B108)
10. Final Judgment (B109)

Derek Prince Ministries
www.derekprince.com

DPM – South Africa
P. O. Box 33367
Glenstantia 0010 Pretoria,
South Africa
T: +27 12 348 9537
E: enquiries@derekprince.co.za
W: www.derekprince.co.za

DPM – Switzerland
Alpenblick 8
CH-8934 Knonau,
Switzerland
T: + 41(0) 44 768 25 06
E: dpm-ch@ibl-dpm.net
W: www.ibl-dpm.net

DPM – UK
PO Box 393,
Hitchin, SG5 9EU
UK
T: + 44 (0) 1462 492100
E: enquiries@dpmuk.org
W: www.dpmuk.org

DPM – USA
P. O. Box 19501
Charlotte NC 28219,
USA
T: + 1 704 357 3556
E: ContactUs@derekprince.org
W: www.derekprince.org

Other books by Derek Prince

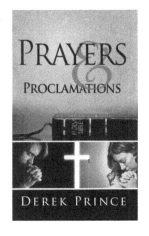

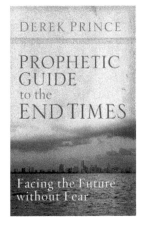

Derek Prince Ministries
Offices Worldwide

DPM – Asia/Pacific
38 Hawdon Street, Sydenham
Christchurch 8023,
New Zealand
T: + 64 3 366 4443
E: admin@dpm.co.nz
W: www.dpm.co.nz and
www.derekprince.in

DPM – Australia
Unit 21/317-321
Woodpark Road, Smithfield
New South Wales 2165,
Australia
T: + 612 9604 0670
E: enquiries@derekprince.com.au
W: www.derekprince.com.au

DPM – Canada
P. O. Box 8354 Halifax,
Nova Scotia B3K 5M1,
Canada
T: + 1 902 443 9577
E: enquiries.dpm@eastlink.ca
W: www.derekprince.org

DPM – France
B.P. 31, Route d'Oupia,
34210 Olonzac,
France
T: + 33 468 913872
E: info@derekprince.fr
W: www.derekprince.fr

DPM – Germany
Söldenhofstr. 10,
83308 Trostberg,
Germany
T: + 49-8621-64146
E: IBL.de@t-online.de
W: www.ibl-dpm.net

DPM – Netherlands
Nobelstraat 7-08
7131 PZ
Lichtenvoorde
Phone: (+31) 251-255044
E: info@dpmnederland.nl
W: www.derekprince.nl

DPM – Norway
P. O. Box 129
Lodderfjord
N-5881, Bergen,
Norway
T: +47 928 39855
E: sverre@derekprince.no
W: www.derekprince.no

Derek Prince Publications Pte. Ltd.
P. O. Box 2046,
Robinson Road Post Office,
Singapore 904046
T: + 65 6392 1812
E: dpmchina@singnet.com.sg
English web: www.dpmchina.org
Chinese web: www.ygmweb.org